STRAIGHT TALKING ABOUT DRUGS

Ecstasy

Sean Connolly

W

FRANKLIN WATTS
LONDON•SYDNEY

An Appleseed Editions book

First published in 2006 by Franklin Watts
338 Euston Road, London NW1 3BH

Franklin Watts Australia
Hachette Children's Books
Level 17/207 Kent St, Sydney, NSW 2000

© 2006 Appleseed Editions

Created by Appleseed Editions Ltd,
Well House, Friars Hill, Guestling,
East Sussex TN35 4ET

Designed by Guy Callaby
Edited by Pip Morgan
Artwork by Karen Donnelly
Picture research by Cathy Tatge

ISBN 0 7496 6756 7

Dewey Classification: 362.29' 9

A CIP catalogue for this book is available from
the British Library.

Photograph acknowledgements
Photographs by Alamy (Everynight Images, David Hoffman Photo
Library, Panacea Pictures, reichhold, DAVID SWINDELLS, Dougie
Wallace), Guy Callaby, Getty Images (Paula Bronstein, Matt Cardy,
Robert E Daemmrich, Bill Eppridge / Time & Life Pictures, Express /
Express, Sean Garnsworthy, Paul Howell, BAY ISMOYO / AFP, ALAIN
JULIEN / AFP, Leelu, Ryan McVay, Matthew Naythons / Liaison,
Network Photographers, Justin Pumfrey, Spencer Rowell, Michael
Smith / Newsmakers, John Stanton, STR / AFP, Time Life Pictures /
Time Magazine, Copyright Time Inc., Julian Wasser / Time Life
Pictures, U.S. Customs / Newsmakers, VCL / Allstair Berg,
Ian Waldie)
Front cover photograph by Getty Images (Stuart McClymont)

Printed in China

Contents

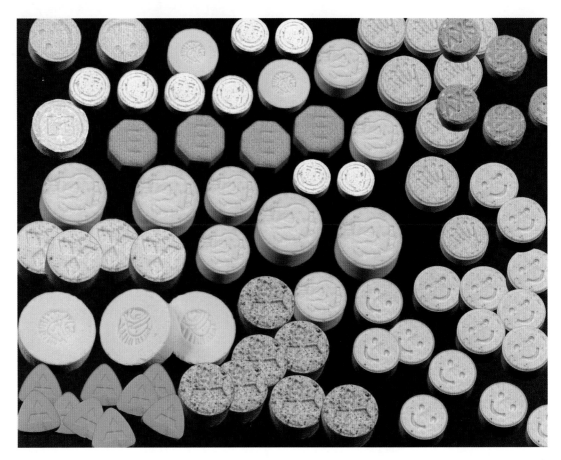

The smiling faces and other designs on ecstasy pills are like brand names. They give clues about who made them and where.

Have you ever enjoyed a good time so much you wished it could go on forever? Or maybe you couldn't stop laughing with a friend because the joke you shared went on and on being funny. Imagine there was a pill you could take that would give you the same feeling again and again, whenever you wanted.

People are trying to do just that when they take a tablet of the illegal drug ecstasy. The active chemical in ecstasy appears to trick the brain into making people feel good, often for hours on end.

Ecstasy also makes their senses, such as hearing and touch, more sensitive. They get more enjoyment from music, especially music with a pulse, and their muscles seem to be itching to move their bodies in time with the beat. All the while they feel happy to be in a crowd and to enjoy the company of whoever is near them.

Paying the price

Wouldn't it be wonderful to take a pill that would make the world a happy and exciting place? But it would be like leaping into the unknown because no-one seems to know how it works. So is the idea too good to be true? The answer is yes, because the body pays a price for staying tuned in to feelings that normally last no more than a few minutes.

People have been taking ecstasy for about 20 years, which is not enough time to study its long-term side-effects and find out how dangerous they are. This is one reason why the drug remains illegal. Some problems are becoming clear, not just in the way ecstasy affects the body, but also in how it works on the brain.

Despite what some ecstasy supporters say – for example, that it is no more dangerous than eating certain popular foods – some serious problems are already obvious. Ecstasy speeds up the heart, raises body temperature and makes the brain work really hard. These effects can increase the chances of a stroke, heart attack or physical collapse.

This all-night beach party in Thailand is the kind of place where ecstasy first became popular. Many people still link ecstasy with dance parties lasting for hours.

" *If you're not on E, it's really scary. The first time I ever went... there were all these people making all these weird faces, and lifting each other off the ground, and pulling each other's arms, and rubbing each other's backs, and jumping around the place like lunatics, and I didn't know what was going on. I'd never been anywhere like that before.* **"**

Natasha, an Irish teenager, describing how ecstasy users enjoy physical contact and giving each other rub-downs.

We have all read books or seen films about mad scientists creating powerful new drugs in their laboratories. Usually, the truth is very different. Teams of scientists work for months or years, making slight changes to familiar substances and then testing them carefully to see what effects the changed substance might have. Many medical advances have come about as a result of this patient teamwork.

Every now and then, scientists create something with unexpected or bewildering effects. The powerful drug LSD, for example, was developed in the 1930s by Swiss scientists who were looking for a treatment for the common cold. The drug we know as ecstasy has a similar story.

Taking an ecstasy pill can be a leap into the unknown, especially in the darkness of a rave or party.

A truth drug?

In 1912, German scientists looking for a drug to stop bleeding developed a chemical called methylenedioxy methamphetamine — MDMA for short. It was patented by the German drugs company Merck, but the company's scientists did not have time to examine the full effects of the new drug because the First World War started. In fact, no one took much interest in MDMA for decades.

It was during a very different war, the tense Cold War, that the US Army began testing MDMA for military purposes. People now believe that, during the 1950s, the army was looking for a drug that would force prisoners to tell the truth. But it didn't work and once again the drug was forgotten.

A British newspaper reporter looks on as a doctor tries out a possible truth drug on a volunteer in 1945.

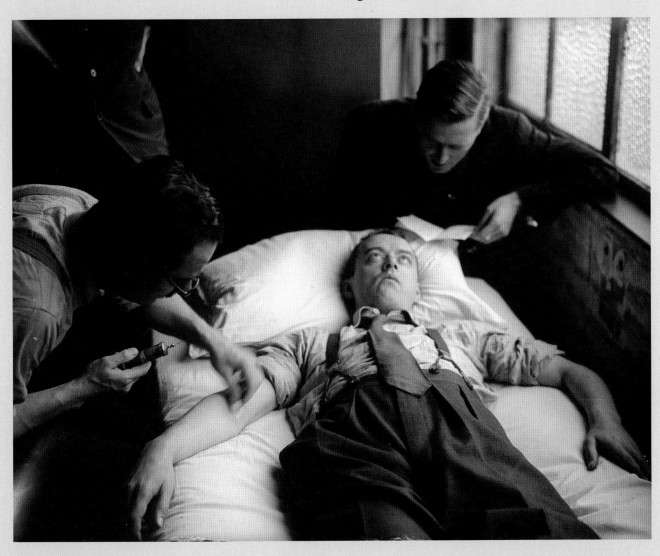

" As [the effects] began dropping away after about an hour and a half... I found myself thinking that I'd been in a remarkable place which I would probably visit again. But first I wanted to find out more about what happens to MDMA in me and what happens to me as a consequence of that interaction. **"**

Dr Alexander Shulgin, recording his experiments with MDMA (ecstasy) in the 1960s.

Many people experimented with mind-changing drugs at the Woodstock music festival in 1969.

New awareness

The 1960s were very different from previous decades as far as drugs were concerned. Millions of people, especially young people, experimented with drugs that altered their minds or changed their moods. They did this just for fun or as a way of uncovering some of the basic truths that were locked inside their brains.

Scientists began investigating how drugs might help people with mental problems. Dr Alexander Shulgin, the American scientist often described as the stepfather of ecstasy, began studying MDMA by taking the drug himself and recording his reactions. He found that MDMA seemed to help unlock the troubling secrets in people's minds by making them more open and relaxed. Shulgin passed his findings on to other psychologists and, like a tossed stone spreading ripples in a pond, the news about MDMA spread through the scientific community – and beyond.

A TYPICAL HIGH

No two people experience a drug in the same way. For example, after a few pints of beer some people become giggly whereas others turn angry or depressed. People's reactions to ecstasy also differ, but in a less extreme way.

Soon after taking ecstasy, people begin to feel tingling sensations and little rushes of excited happiness. Occasionally, they feel sick or dizzy, too, but this soon wears off. Regular users call this first stage 'coming up'.

> *After around 45 minutes the first subtle effects began – I started to feel light-headed and my whole body started to tingle gently. I felt an urge to stretch my arms and legs – rather as one does when waking up after a good night's sleep.*

British ecstasy user describing his first ecstasy experience.

In the first two hours, the effects come in powerful waves, each stronger than the last. Users feel more open and relaxed in each other's company and are often more sensitive to touch. The peak lasts for between four and six hours. The effects gradually wear off (the stage known as coming down) for about two more hours.

Many users find their jaws clench or clamp so they chew gum or a dummy, or suck lollies or smoke cigarettes.

Dr Benjamin Weininger (right) leads a 1974 training session for people learning how to be psychological counsellors.

MDMA burst on to the world scene and gained its more familiar name ecstasy in the 1970s and 1980s. It all started with a type of treatment designed to help people with psychological problems. During the 1970s, psychologists and other mental health professionals gave their patients various drugs to help them open up and talk about themselves and the problems they faced.

Unlocking secrets

Patients often defend themselves by fighting any attempt to unlock the secrets that trouble them. Psychologists realized that MDMA was a way of overcoming that defence because it seemed to give some patients the chance to face inner problems they would normally ignore or hide. At the same time, though, they worried that the drug would be made illegal if the wider public began using it frequently – if only because its side-effects were not fully known.

At this point MDMA was not yet known as ecstasy. The American chemists who produced it legally sometimes called it Adam because they believed that the drug helped people return to the purer world of the biblical Adam, living peacefully in the Garden of Eden.

↑ Followers of Indian mystic Bhagwan Shree Rajneesh take part in a ritual session in 1984 to rid themselves of feelings of greed and selfishness. They often took ecstasy to help this process.

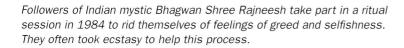 **It was a new type of action. I found myself able to remain completely clear, completely lucid, I had excellent recall. I had none of the cloudiness of recall that sometimes does come with some of the delusional drugs. None of that was there at all. I found myself being able to think honestly.** 🗨

Dr Alexander Shulgin describing his experiences with ecstasy, inspiring others to follow his example.

The first people to use MDMA as a recreational drug thought it could help them think and develop. Many took it with a few friends in a familiar setting, such as a living room. Although we now know that MDMA is at least partly a stimulant, these people took it to relax and to look inwards.

Another group of users were followers of Bhagwan Shree Rajneesh, a mystic from India who attracted many people to his way of life. These people came to be known as sanyassins, which is based on a Sanskrit word meaning complete or perfect abandonment (of worldly goods). Ecstasy was an important step for many sanyassins in their journey to rid themselves of the unnecessary clutter of modern life. They travelled from the USA to Europe to spread the Bhagwan's message. At the same time, they helped to spread the use of ecstasy.

Ecstasy is born

By the late 1970s and early 1980s, more than 4,000 American psychologists were using MDMA with their patients. Word began to leak out that this new wonder drug could combine some of the mind-changing effects of illegal drugs such as LSD, cannabis and amphetamines. Because the drug was still legal, it was being manufactured and carried across the USA. People in Texas, one of the drug's distribution centres, could even buy MDMA freely in bars. Other Americans could order it over the phone.

The next step was hardly surprising. Some of the people involved in making and distributing MDMA saw that there was a huge market for the drug outside the world of mental health care. They believed that many more people would like to take MDMA themselves, without having to visit a professional for a psychological consultation. In fact, they felt that MDMA was not only exciting, it was fun. The only drawback was that its official name sounded too scientific.

WHAT IS GOING ON?

Like other drugs that change people's moods, ecstasy alters the way chemicals work inside the brain. In particular, it affects the way nerve cells send and receive the chemicals serotonin and dopamine, which affect people's moods.

Serotonin acts as a messenger between the brain's nerve cells and helps to regulate a person's mood and appetite. Dopamine is the chemical that rewards us with pleasurable experiences. Normally, these two chemicals are sent through the brain in short bursts. But ecstasy causes them to remain for several hours and they flood the brain's nerve cells. Before the brain eventually breaks down these chemicals, the sense of pleasure and relaxation – so famous with ecstasy – lingers for the person who has taken the drug.

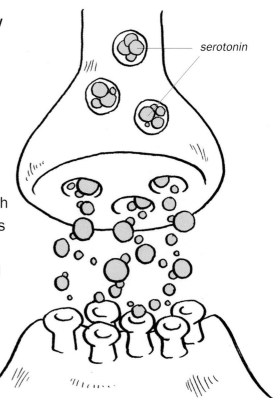

serotonin

In 1981 in Los Angeles, an MDMA distributor (whose name remains secret) invented a name for MDMA that sounded less chemical and so would attract more buyers and users. He gave it the nickname ecstasy (which means a state of sudden and extreme delight), although he later admitted that a more accurate name for the drug would be empathy. This other term, which he felt few people would know, describes a feeling of friendship and understanding between people – a feeling that keeps many people taking the drug.

A joyful sense of celebration expresses the empathy that people can share.

SEARCHING QUESTION
If governments had acted faster and banned ecstasy as soon as they learned about its dangers, would scientists have been angry because they hadn't had a chance to explore it?

Dancers at a rave may take ecstasy to heighten their feelings and to help them continue for hours on end.

Ecstasy was discovered in Germany, used medically and then for pleasure in the USA, but exploded on to the world stage in Britain and Spain in the mid-1980s. Many young British people were already familiar with the stimulants speed and cocaine (which boosted energy) and the hallucinogen LSD (which made feelings more intense). Now they heard about ecstasy, which seemed to be a combination of both – without any obvious side-effects and with a high that lasted for hours.

Before long, many young people were taking ecstasy, which also gave birth to a new style of music and partying. Slang terms such as sorted (having got hold of some ecstasy) set these people apart from those who hadn't heard of – or chose not to take – ecstasy.

WHY DANCING?

Just what is it about ecstasy that makes people want to get up and dance? Why do the most famous ecstasy-related dance events – raves – go on for hours on end? The answer lies in the way that the drug affects the mind and body. Ecstasy makes people comfortable in each other's company and eager to share experiences. People experience things – sounds in particular – more strongly. The tingling feeling in their muscles makes them want to move about. The drug's effects on the brain last for many hours, which is the reason why raves go on all night.

" Party drug [mainly ecstasy] use started in the rave community in the late 1980s and early 90s and now it has spread out into the mainstream of youth culture. Drug use is regarded as a normal part of young people's leisure time, of going out and dancing. "

Cameron Duff of the Australian Drug Foundation's Centre for Youth Drug Studies.

The smiley face, already a popular emblem, became linked with the ecstasy boom in the 1980s and 1990s.

Summer of love

Millions of Britons travel to southern Europe every summer in search of sun and entertainment. Some resorts, such as the Spanish island of Ibiza, are particularly popular with younger people. It was on Ibiza that young drug users began taking ecstasy in large amounts in the mid-1980s. A drug that promised hours of happiness and warm feelings seemed ideal for all-night parties under Spanish skies.

A new style of intense, repetitive dance music, known as Acid House, blossomed in Ibiza's clubs. Hundreds of T-shirts with smiley faces signalled the number of people high on the happy drug at raves. Each year saw more smiley faces and more pounding music lasting through the night. The peak year was 1988, which ravers called the second summer of love – the first was in 1967, when young people discovered LSD.

www.time.com   AOL Keyword: TIME

EXCLUSIVE:
Barak on Why Israel Left Lebanon

TIME

WHAT
ECSTASY
DOES TO YOUR BRAIN
■ The Science
■ The Rave Scene
■ Inside a Crime Ring

0 925675 0

The American news magazine Time
*devoted a cover story to ecstasy and
its risks in 2000.*

Into the clubs

Ibiza ravers returned to Britain with a taste for the new music – and the new drug that seemed to go with it so well. They started going to raves – illegal all-night dance parties held in empty warehouses and fields. The police and local councils grew concerned about these raves, not only because of the drugs, but also because of safety concerns (fires were always a threat) and complaints about noise from local people. New laws were introduced that gave harsher penalties to people who created disturbances with pulsating music.

The authorities wanted people to gather in places that met basic health and safety requirements, so nightclubs were allowed to remain open all night. Clubs such as the Hacienda in Manchester and the Ministry of Sound in London, which recreated the sounds and experience of ecstasy-fuelled raves on Ibiza, became very popular and set the example for others in Britain. Other young people were spreading a similar message in Amsterdam, Berlin, Milan and other cities across Europe. The ecstasy boom had begun.

> **" Every week we used nearly all our money. We'd get into debt on a Saturday night, we'd get out of it on a Friday night and we'd get back into it on a Saturday night. It'd be the same thing every single week. "**

Cory, a teenager from Cork, Ireland, describing how she spent most of her weekly earnings on buying ecstasy.

Raves continue to be popular in the 21st century. This photograph shows some of the 40,000 people who attended the Teknival rave in northern France in April 2005.

SEARCHING QUESTION

Do you think products such as smiley T-shirts, which seem to support taking ecstasy, should be illegal?

Many dancers know about the effects of dehydration so they always carry a bottle of water.

Rave culture proved to be a powerful force in the 1980s and 1990s. More and more young people began taking ecstasy – in the UK, Europe, North America, Australia and wherever people could assemble a sound system and organize a rave.

Nothing seemed to stand in the way of ecstasy's popularity – even drug experts were caught by surprise. Then, in 1995, the tragic death of a young English girl dramatically changed the public's view of ecstasy. Eighteen-year-old Leah Betts took an ecstasy pill at an Essex nightclub and later fell into a coma, from which she never recovered.

Leah's story captured the British imagination and was used as an example of how illegal drugs, especially ecstasy, can kill. The Betts family approved advertisements showing a photograph of Leah with the headline "Sorted: just one ecstasy tablet killed Leah Betts". It later turned out that Leah had not died from ecstasy directly. Instead, her body had stopped working after she had drunk as much as seven litres of water in about 90 minutes (ecstasy users often become dehydrated). Despite what was said in some of the publicity, the pill she took that night was not her first. These facts, though, were overlooked amid the widespread fears about ecstasy.

More than a decade has passed since Leah Bett's death. During that time other young people have died, either from taking ecstasy itself or because of complications that developed after taking it.

Chinese actors show a young woman being spirited away to a life of drug dependence in this performance at a bar in the eastern city of Hangzhou in 2003.

ECSTASY TERMS

Below are some slang terms commonly used in the UK when talking about ecstasy.

Banging tunes Loud music with a strong beat that sounds good when taking ecstasy.

Chilled tunes Tranquil music that sounds good when taking ecstasy – usually put on in the early hours of the morning.

Coming up Beginning to feel the effects of an ecstasy pill.

Come down The next day as the effects are wearing off.

Double drop To take two ecstasy pills at once.

E Ecstasy.

Go half To divide a pill in half and share with a friend.

Luvdup Wanting to love/hug everyone as a result of taking ecstasy.

Mashed/muntered State of mind when someone has taken a few pills.

On a mission In search of ecstasy tablets.

Pilling one's socks off Having taken a lot of ecstasy.

Pill head A person who takes a lot of ecstasy regularly.

Popped/necked Having taken an ecstasy pill.

Sorted Having bought ecstasy pills in time for the weekend.

Inside Glastonbury

Every year more than 100,000 music lovers make their way to Somerset to attend the three-day Glastonbury Festival, Europe's largest musical event. One of the biggest Glastonbury attractions is the Dance Tent – an organized rave that many people link with ecstasy use.

Michael Eavis, the owner of Worthy Farm (the festival site), is aware that there are probably drugs on site. Careful medical preparations each year help him to deal with overheating, dehydration and other ecstasy-related problems. He even has sunblock for sunny days. Medical teams also help people with the psychological side-effects of drugs, especially those created by LSD and ecstasy.

Eavis points out that being prepared for drug problems is not the same as approving drug use. "We have medical staff and people handing out water in the Dance Tent, and emergency services are on hand elsewhere on the site."

He beleives that the music, the crowds and the overall atmosphere provide the real buzz at the festival. "Experimenting with drugs might seem exciting to some young people there, but what seems exciting when you're not on drugs can become bewildering and alarming if you are. You could be ruining more than your festival if you do it – it's just not worth it."

Dancers need to refresh themselves regularly by drinking water, even when it rains at Glastonbury Festival.

❝ *I did E for the first time when I was 12, because my friend's older brother was doing it, and I wanted to be cool and fit in. Once you start [using drugs] you don't stop, and once you get into that crowd that uses drugs you don't want to. You feel like that's where you fit in, and anybody that doesn't do drugs isn't cool enough for you to hang out with.* **❞**

Ashley, interviewed on US TV about ecstasy use.

In 2005, the Dancer Village at Glastonbury handed out headphones for the Silent Disco, which lasted from 1 am to 6 am every day.

SEARCHING QUESTION
Do you think that the Glastonbury Festival and other events popular with young people should play a more active role in persuading people not to take ecstasy?

"I'm addicted to chocolate." "My cousin is a TV soap addict." "He'd do better at school if he could overcome his addiction to computer games." We hear the word addiction, or forms of it, nearly every day. We usually mean that the person cannot stop doing something which is either harmful or expensive.**

Many people become overwhelmed by an uncontrollable urge to do something, or to continue doing something, that they feel is wrong. They are unable to stop. Doctors and psychologists who try to help them recognize these urges, but instead of using the words addict or addiction they refer to this type of behaviour as dependence.

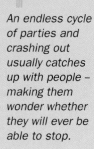

An endless cycle of parties and crashing out usually catches up with people – making them wonder whether they will ever be able to stop.

Many regular ecstasy users find it hard to return to work after the weekend. Their depressed and confused state is sometimes called a Black Monday.

Two types of dependence

People can become dependent on drugs in two main ways. First is physical dependence, when the body becomes so used to a substance that a person needs to take it just to get through the day. Nicotine (the drug in tobacco) and alcohol can both produce physical dependence. When the body no longer receives the substance, it goes into withdrawal. People who are physically dependent on a drug, especially alcohol and heroin, have great difficulty overcoming withdrawal symptoms and so find it hard to break their habit.

The second type of dependence is psychological. A person who stops taking a substance does not have hallucinations, fever or nausea (as they would if they were physically dependent). Instead, they feel a craving for the missing substance. The problem might be all in the mind, but it doesn't make it any easier to overcome.

Where does ecstasy fit into this picture?

FERGIE'S ECSTASY HABIT

Black Eyed Peas singer Fergie was once dependent on ecstasy and other drugs. She began taking ecstasy in her 20s and was soon taking it regularly. As her ecstasy habit grew, she started experimenting with harder drugs.

Interviewed by *Cosmopolitan* magazine, Fergie said: "My life was falling apart. I owed a lot of money and was going out of my mind imagining things. I went into a downward spiral and hit rock bottom." It was only through the help of close friends and a course of counselling that Fergie was able to overcome her problems, rebuild her life and make way for ultimate success.

" It's not just teenagers who are being silly. It's also people in their 20s and 30s. The sad ones are the really young teenagers. I don't know where they get their supply from, but there seems to be absolutely no shortage, they have no difficulty in obtaining it. "

Gordon Fulde, director of emergency services at St Vincent's Hospital in Sydney, Australia.

Tolerating ecstasy

There is no real evidence that people become physically dependent on ecstasy. However, some regular users feel depressed or anxious when they stop taking it, so there may be some psychological dependence.

People who are dependent on a substance often become used to it and so need larger amounts to reach the same highs. This is called tolerance. For example, people who are dependent on alcohol usually build up such a tolerance: they need five or six drinks to feel the same effects that one or two gave them before. People can build up a tolerance to ecstasy as well. A person who takes ecstasy regularly does not feel the same happy buzz from one tablet as those who are taking it for the first time.

As a person builds a tolerance to ecstasy, a single pill no longer provides the same rush or high – and the habit can grow as a result.

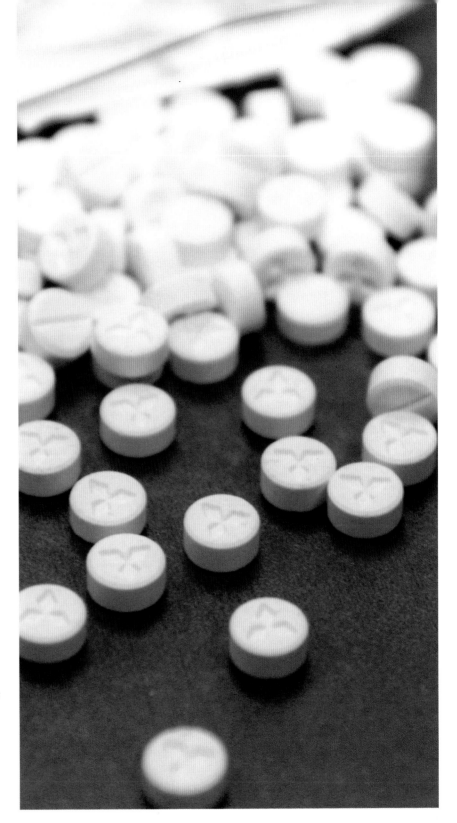

SEARCHING QUESTION
Can you think of anything that you are dependent on? What about your friends or family members?

The dangers of ecstasy

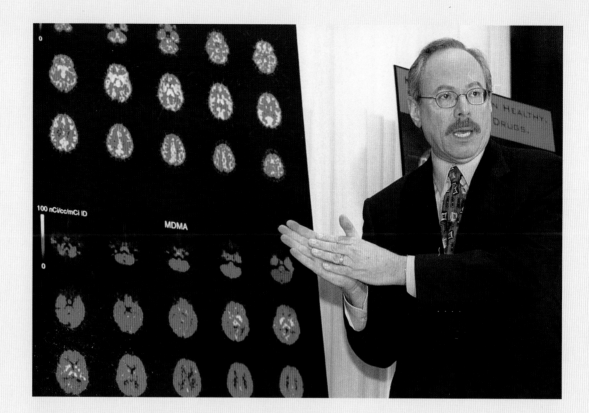

People are unsure about the dangers of ecstasy. Some demand that controls be strengthened because of the tragic deaths related to it. Others say it is much safer than legal drugs such as alcohol. What does seem clear is that taking ecstasy can cause problems, and those who are likely to use it or be with those who take it should know the full story.

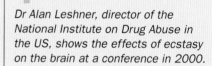

Dr Alan Leshner, director of the National Institute on Drug Abuse in the US, shows the effects of ecstasy on the brain at a conference in 2000.

" *I have been going to raves and taking E for just over a year. Though I don't take E every weekend, I have still taken it quite often. Last weekend I had gone to a party with my friends and had returned to a friend's house to watch the sun rise, spin, drink, and so on. However, this did not turn out to be a normal morning after. I had a seizure. The last thing I remember was being outside on the deck, the next thing I knew is that I was in an ambulance and had an IV in my arm and wires were everywhere.* "

First-hand account posted on www.ecstasy.org

HOW ECSTASY CAN KILL

Most experts agree there are three main ways people can die from ecstasy. Australia's Young Adult Health website describes them and explains what might be done to avoid them.

1 The victims drown their brain. This happens when they drink too much water and the excess fluid affects their brain. **Take regular sips of water rather than drinking large amounts at once. Half a litre per hour is recommended.**

2 Ecstasy can cause a heart attack or brain haemorrhage. You can't stop this happening. **It just depends on how your body reacts. This is a risk you take if you choose to use ecstasy.**

3 Overheating. Taking ecstasy and dancing for a long time raises your body temperature to dangerous levels. You are usually somewhere hot, too. Your muscles can become exhausted. **Chill out regularly. Have a rest from dancing. Hang out somewhere cool and wear light clothes to keep you cool (in every sense of the word).**

DEAD SAFE
Supporters of ecstasy point out that the death rate from using the drug is seven for every million users each year. This means that taking ecstasy is safer than fishing or eating peanuts.

The loved-up feelings that many ecstasy users express can hide some of the physical dangers they face in taking the drug.

EMERGENCY ACTION

Australia's Child and Youth Health website publishes the following clear advice about how to deal with someone who has had a bad experience at a rave or in another setting where ecstasy is involved.

● Get help – call an ambulance.

● Stay with the person; talk with them; find out if he or she is conscious.

● Do not move them, unless you need to keep them safe.

● Clear a space around them. It is critical to be honest when you seek medical attention. Give the ambulance staff and doctors information about what drugs have been taken. The truth might save a life!

Ecstasy users – and those around them – need to be aware that a bad experience with the drug can lead to emergency medical treatment.

> **" The short-term [risks] are worrying too. I don't like the hangover. If I have a big weekend I can get really tearful on the Tuesday or Wednesday for no reason, or I get really snappy. But not everyone thinks like that. It's so cheap now that some people are downing them like there's no tomorrow. "**

Patrick, a regular ecstasy user, interviewed in a London club.

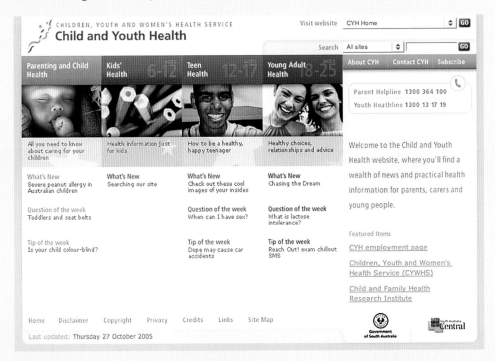

Public-health websites offer a wide range of practical advice on how to deal with the medical risks of ecstasy and other drugs.

> **" In America, users seem to be more aware that there are dangers with ecstasy. But in the UK, especially among 15–24-year-old users who take it quite a lot, there is a lack of awareness of what it may result in later. "**

Lynn Taurah, psychology researcher at London Metropolitan University.

STUDYING ECSTASY

Most research into the long-term effects of ecstasy concentrates on the brain, especially the memory. A Dutch study in 2001, led by Dr Liesbeth Renemen of the Academic Medical Centre, Amsterdam, examined brain cells from 69 volunteers.

The volunteers were put into four groups: non-users, moderate users (who had taken fewer than 55 tablets in their lives), heavy users and ex-users (who had taken their last tablet a year before the tests).

The results showed that heavy users had lost more of the cells that rely on serotonin to communicate within the brain (see pages 14–15), and that women had lost more than men. The same parts of the brain had begun to recover among the ex-users, but they were worse than non-users in basic memory tests.

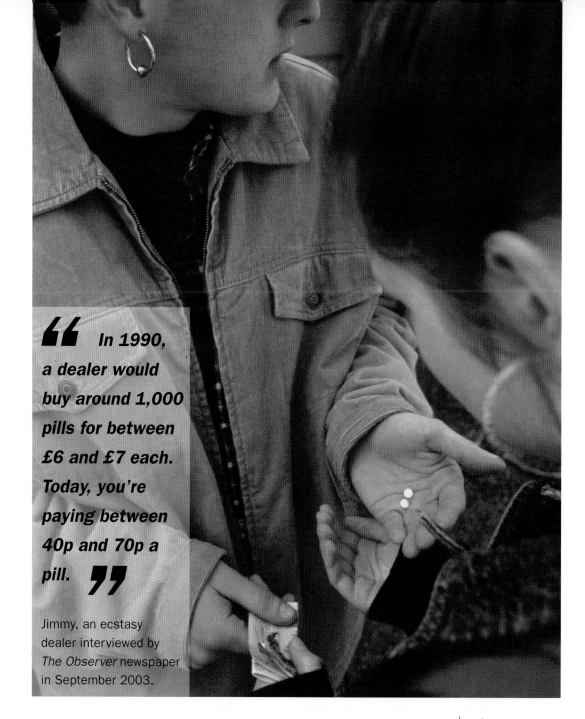

> **In 1990, a dealer would buy around 1,000 pills for between £6 and £7 each. Today, you're paying between 40p and 70p a pill.**
>
> Jimmy, an ecstasy dealer interviewed by *The Observer* newspaper in September 2003.

People who manufacture, distribute and sell ecstasy make profits just like those involved with vitamin pills. The big difference, of course, is that they do it illegally. They pay no tax on their earnings and risk facing huge fines or prison sentences if they are caught.

The big difference for their customers (the people who buy and take the ecstasy) is that there is no guarantee that the ecstasy tablets are pure. An ecstasy buyer cannot be sure how much of the tablet, if any, is made up of ecstasy. Many tablets are doctored with cheap substances such as aspirin. Others include different drugs, such as LSD and ketamine, with effects that often come as an unpleasant and dangerous surprise.

A woman pays a dealer for ecstasy. How can she be sure that the white tablets are what she thinks they are?

The ecstasy business

Ecstasy is a complicated drug to make and the buyer is several steps removed from the source of the drug (see right). The ecstasy business is worth millions of pounds and works like a pyramid. At the top are the producers, who invest a lot of money in equipment and ingredients. They sell large amounts of the drug to distributors, who import it into different countries. Each distributor then sells the ecstasy to larger numbers of people who act as dealers (the people who sell the tablets to users).

Many of the customers are people who buy it regularly and rely on a particular dealer they believe they can trust. Others are simply curious or eager to try something forbidden – or even dangerous. Some of these first-time buyers have decided to buy and take ecstasy because of peer pressure. They believe they won't be cool or accepted by their friends if they refuse to take the drug.

SKYROCKETING USE

A detailed report published by the United Nations Office on Drugs and Crime in 2003 produced some staggering statistics about the widespread use of ecstasy. The research showed that in the UK:

● *2.2 per cent of the population aged 16 to 59 take ecstasy regularly, compared with 1.2 per cent in 1998.*

● *The total number of ecstasy users (730,000 people) is set to overtake the combined number of people who take cocaine and heroin.*

● *More people take ecstasy as a proportion of the population than in any other country, except Australia and Ireland.*

● *More than 120 million tonnes of ecstasy are now produced annually.*

● *This mass production has led to a drop in prices: an ecstasy tablet can be bought for £3.*

GROWING PROFITS

Ecstasy is made from ingredients that are changed chemically in the production process. The following steps show how the costs – and eventual profits –grow at each step of the process:

● *£30: the amount growers are paid for every kilogram of essential oil extracted from the bark of the sassafras tree.*

● *Companies based in China and other countries convert the oil into the chemical piperonyl for legal uses such as pesticides and perfumes. Piperonyl, however, is also the raw ingredient for ecstasy.*

● *£65 per kilogram: fake companies buy the piperonyl, pretending to want it for legal uses.*

● *£1,000–£4,000 per kilogram: ecstasy factories, mostly in Belgium, Luxembourg, the Netherlands and Eastern Europe then buy the piperonyl.*

● *These factories process the piperonyl with other chemicals to create MDMA powder, which is then formed into tablets.*

● *£20,000–£40,000 per kilogram: dealers buy the MDMA (a kilogram of MDMA can create 10,000 pills).*

● *£30,000–£50,000: street value of a kilogram of ecstasy tablets if each pill is sold for £3–5.*

From The Observer,
28 September 2003

SEARCHING QUESTION
Would you buy something if you couldn't be sure what it was?

Ecstasy is illegal and most people recognize that it poses a risk to those who take it. That much is easy to agree, but experts disagree on how to control its use. Some people favour strict penalties to deter people from taking ecstasy; others believe that better education and treatment is the answer. No one wants badly informed ecstasy users to risk their lives.

Ecstasy and schools

Many people believe that schools should play an important role in the war against drugs. In their view, schools should not just teach children about drugs and their effects; they should actively seek out and punish those who take illegal drugs. One approach, which is widespread in America, is known as zero tolerance. Under this policy, children found with illegal drugs such as ecstasy face immediate expulsion from school. The policy sometimes extends to areas surrounding school property.

Australian model Michelle Leslie returns to Sydney on 22 November 2005 after being expelled from Indonesia, where she had spent three months in prison for possessing ecstasy.

THE LEGAL POSITION

Ecstasy is illegal in nearly every country. It can be detected in a person's urine for about two to four days. In the UK, ecstasy is a Class A drug, which is the most serious classification (heroin and cocaine are also Class A drugs). This means that:

● People found with one ecstasy pill may receive only a caution from the police.

● Being caught with more than one pill is a serious matter. The police sometimes charge the user with intent to supply (which means they are aiming to sell the drug), even if they only meant to give their extra pills to friends.

● Being convicted of supplying ecstasy can lead to a sentence of life imprisonment and an unlimited fine.

The legal position in Australia is more complicated. Some drug laws are nationwide and others are enforced by an individual state. The position in New South Wales (and Australia's largest city, Sydney) is that:

● People being caught with small amounts of ecstasy (fewer than 15 tablets) face a fine of up to A$3,000 or one year in prison or both.

● Those convicted of drug trafficking face a fine of A$15,000 or 15 years' imprisonment, or both.

● People convicted of drug trafficking to a minor face a fine of up to A$250,000 or 20 years' imprisonment, or both.

● Commercial (large-scale) drug trafficking convictions carry fines of up to A$250,000 or 25 years' imprisonment or both.

Class A drugs are regularly seized by police and customs officials in the war against traffickers.

Random testing

Another weapon in the war on drugs is random drug testing. A school randomly chooses a group of children every week and tests them for drugs. At present, UK schools can randomly test children if the school and parents agree. In 2005, the UK Home Secretary Charles Clarke supported random testing and suggested that it could soon become law.

In January 2005, the Abbey School in Faversham, Kent, became the first school to randomly test children. Every Wednesday, the mouth of each pupil is rubbed with a cotton swab. A computer chooses 20 names and those children's swabs are sent to a drug-testing laboratory. If any test is positive (indicating drugs) the child is not expelled, but is questioned to find out how they got hold of the drug. Peter Walker, the headteacher, stressed that no-one would be forced to take the drug test. He also said that random testing would reduce peer pressure to take drugs since anyone could be caught.

 One of the difficulties we have in our society is that the government has tried so hard and so much to try to improve levels of prevention, yet we are not meeting with enough success.

Peter Walker, headteacher at the Abbey School, Kent, after introducing random drug testing.

More than 60 schools in Texas use professional dog handlers to search for drugs in students' lockers and other places on campus. The dogs sit down if they sniff drugs, alcohol or even gunpowder.

Indonesian police officials display more than 23,000 seized ecstasy tablets before destroying them at police headquarters in the capital, Jakarta, in 2003. Indonesia has introduced stronger anti-drug policies. Dealers in ecstasy and other drugs face harsh penalties – and even death – if they are convicted.

HARM REDUCTION

One approach to dealing with drugs such as ecstasy is known as harm reduction. This means that governments and drug-awareness groups concentrate more on educating the public about drugs generally and less on arresting people with a drug.

Supporters argue that, in the case of ecstasy, fewer people would suffer from overheating, dehydration and the effects of mixing drugs.

Opponents say that it sends a signal to people that drugs are OK and that the government and police don't really think drugs are a problem. They also believe that harm reduction leads to wider drug use and a worse problem for the future.

Australia has adopted some harm-reduction measures. Surveys show that 52 per cent of Australians aged 16–29 have taken drugs. Sweden takes a harsher approach to drug use. The proportion of Swedes in the same age group who have taken drugs is only 9 per cent.

SEARCHING QUESTION
Some people say that random drug testing in schools is wrong because it makes teachers do the work of the police. What do you think?

There are signs that ecstasy no longer captures the imagination of young people in the way it did 15 or 20 years ago. Why has this happened?

One simple reason is fashion. Drugs, like clothes and music, go in and out of fashion and young people often reject the fashions of those older than them. So in some ways ecstasy use has followed the micro-scooter and big hair – it has begun to seem less cool.

Another reason is that the cost of ecstasy has fallen. Twenty years ago people would willingly pay £25 for a pill, but today the cost is often below £3, making ecstasy about the same price as a pint of beer. It has lost the attraction of being hard to reach and so special. Just think: would caviar and champagne seem so special if their price dropped by 800 per cent?

For many young people, the smiley face badge now means cheerfulness, rather than being a secret sign that the person is taking ecstasy.

Some ecstasy users start to take cocaine but are unaware of its dangers.

The message gets through

The most likely reason for ecstasy's loss of popularity is the fact that more people know the risks involved. They know about the side–effects but they also know that ecstasy pills might contain a dangerous substance such as liquid ecstasy (see below right).

Recent studies in North America have shown that the numbers of young people trying ecstasy have fallen – although overall ecstasy use has remained steady, or even risen slightly. If this fall continues, it would lead to fewer people taking the drug in the future as many existing users would stop once they settle down with jobs and families.

Monitoring the Future, a nationwide study organized by the University of Michigan Institute for Social Research, asked American teenagers about their views on ecstasy and other drugs. Lloyd Johnson, in charge of the study, believes it shows clear evidence that young people are more alert to the risks of ecstasy. His study found that:

● Only 38 per cent of 17-year-olds interviewed in 2000 believed that there was a great risk of harm linked to trying ecstasy.

● The figure jumped to 46 per cent in 2001.

● In 2002, more than half of those interviewed (52 per cent) were concerned about this great risk of harm.

" *Five years ago, you went to a club to take drugs, dance like a loon and leave at six in the morning. Now it's different; there are lots of different sorts of music. It's a lot more social. Yeah, there are pills there, but you don't have to take them.* **"**

Paul Knight, a London DJ.

NEEDING HELP

In 2002, a study of 1,000 readers of the UK dance magazine Mixmag found that clubbers are twice as likely as others to consult a doctor about mental problems. One in four had symptoms of a psychiatric disorder; others reported problems such as anxiety, insomnia, poor concentration and low self-esteem. One in 10 drug users believed that taking ecstasy had made their lives worse overall.

The survey, overseen by Dr Adam Winstock of the National Addiction Centre at the University of Kent in Canterbury, claims to provide a reliable snapshot of drug-taking on the dance scene, as 98 per cent of those interviewed admitted taking ecstasy and other drugs.

LIQUID ECSTASY

Ecstasy has many fake versions that sellers claim are the real thing – or even better. One of these is usually called liquid ecstasy. This odourless liquid is really a chemical called gamma hydroxybutyrate (GHB), which comes in small bottles that users break open and sniff.

Unlike ecstasy, which is a stimulant, GHB was developed to calm people. In small doses, it makes users feel relaxed and sociable – rather like alcohol. In higher doses, it can cause dizziness, loss of co-ordination – even unconsciousness and death.

Talking in a relaxed setting – with friends or in a family group – is the best way to discuss drugs such as ecstasy.

Many young people become confused and unable to make a sensible judgement when faced with so much conflicting information about ecstasy. On one hand, they are told the buzz is fantastic and that there is more danger from eating peanut butter or going fishing. On the other hand, anti-drugs posters and information make them think that taking just one ecstasy tablet could lead to serious physical and mental problems – and maybe even death.

Unlike children growing up in the 1960s and 1970s, today's young people have parents who also learned about drugs in their youth. Perhaps they are too old to have come across ecstasy as teenagers, but some parents may have taken or been offered cannabis, cocaine and maybe even LSD. They had to make their own minds up about these drugs. Their experiences are valuable. Try talking to them honestly about ecstasy to find out how they feel about it and what advice they can give.

Similarly, youth group leaders, sports coaches and other adults (such as a friendly teacher) may have experiences to draw upon. Most of these people would be pleased to share their views about ecstasy and drugs generally. Finally, talk to and share information with other young people about your concerns – they are probably just as confused as you.

Most young people can enjoy themselves in a group without the need for artificial highs from ecstasy or other drugs.

ADVICE ON THE WEB

Online chat and other websites can help young people share problems, often with others around the world. The following is an edited question and reply from MyDearDiary.com.

Question
I live in Las Vegas where underground raves are common. I have gone to a few and they can be fun. Well, my friend who went with me a few times is now starting to go all the time. I wouldn't care but now she has been taking ecstasy and (I think) having sex with many people. Being that we are only 16, I think she should slow down but she doesn't want to. Does anyone know what ecstasy can do to you?

Reply from Tressie
A lot of the people at my school have moved on from weed [cannabis] to ecstasy. About five of my friends just got expelled for having ecstasy at a dance. Some of them are also being charged on some kind of rape charge because ecstasy is considered a date rape drug...Regular use [of ecstasy] will f*** you up so hard. Well anyways, just tell your friend what you know, try to help her. If she don't listen, just hope for the best for her.

*A library is an ideal place to find out more about ecstasy –
especially for someone worried or embarrassed about
discussing drugs with friends or family members.*

Private investigations

Many young people are embarrassed to bring up
subjects such as drugs and sex with their parents,
or with any adults that they know. If you feel like that,
you can still get useful drug information easily. Your
school or local library probably has books and leaflets
about ecstasy. Try looking for some of the books
listed on pages 44–45 or ask the librarian for advice.
The websites listed at the end of this book have
honest and up-to-date information about ecstasy
and other drugs. Start your own private investigation
and see where it leads.

JUST SAY KNOW

Ecstasy is a young person's drug, so much information comes via mobile phone calls, text messages and the Internet. The information often includes how and where to buy ecstasy, when and where raves are planned and other news about the drug.

Some young people have begun using the same channels to pass on good advice about ecstasy and other drugs. RaveSafe, a website set up by a group of South Africans in 1994, acts as a noticeboard for the drug scene. The site provides detailed information about ecstasy and has links to other sites dealing with scientific, legal and health issues. The aim is to allow people to make informed decisions about drugs. RaveSafe neither supports nor condemns ecstasy. Instead, it operates under the motto 'Just say Know', a pun on the 'Just say No' slogan that many drug control organizations use.

Some people prefer to discuss their concerns about drugs in the free-flowing conversation of a group.

SEARCHING QUESTION
What do you think is the best way to persuade someone not to take ecstasy?

Glossary

amphetamines drugs that work on the body's nervous system to lift a person's mood

caution a police warning that is held for five years in national police records and which can be used against someone if they commit a similar offence

Cold War the period from 1945 to 1990 when the United States and its international supporters were prepared for a war against the Soviet Union (the former government of Russia) and its supporters

coma a long period of unconsciousness caused by illness or injury

dealers people who sell drugs illegally

dehydrated having lost a great deal of the body's water

dilated wider than normal

drug trafficking the legal term for selling illegal drugs

empathy an understanding of other people's moods or problems

expulsion sent away from school permanently

First World War a global conflict, lasting from 1914 to 1918, involving many countries mainly in Europe

haemorrhage a flow of blood from damaged blood vessels

hallucinogen a drug that causes a hallucination, a sensation of something that does not exist outside the mind – for example, imagined sights or sounds

heart attack damage to the heart when it is deprived of oxygen

import to bring something into a country in order to sell it

ketamine a powerful drug that produces hallucinations and in larger doses can cause unconsciousness

LSD a powerful hallucinogen

lucid very clear

minor someone under the age of 18

patent to register an idea or product in a country so that others cannot copy and make money from it

peer pressure persuasion from people your age to do something in order to remain part of the group

pesticide chemicals used by farmers and other people to control pests such as harmful insects, rats, etc

process to prepare or treat something in order to manufacture something else from it

profit the difference between what someone pays to buy or make something and what they charge when they sell it

psychological relating to the mind and how it operates

pulsating beating out a steady rhythm

recreational (in the case of drugs) taken for pleasure rather than for a medical reason

Sanskrit the ancient language of India

seizure a violent and uncontrollable tightening of muscles

stimulants drugs that affect the nervous system to make a person feel more energetic and lively

stroke a blockage of a blood vessel leading to the brain, causing difficulties in speaking and moving. In severe cases, it affects thinking and may even cause death

swab a small stick with a cotton bud at each end

tremors uncontrollable trembling

unco-ordinated unable to control physical movement

withdrawal physical and psychological changes in a person who has stopped taking a substance after developing a dependence on it

Books

The Score: Facts About Drugs (Health Education Authority, London, 1998)

Buzzed: The Straight Facts About the Most Used Drugs from Alcohol to Ecstasy C. Kuhn. (W. W. Norton & Co, Ltd, 2003)

Drugs: the Truth (Teenage Health Freak) A. Macfarlane and A. McPherson. (Oxford University Press, 2003)

Drugs A. Naik. (Hodder Children's Books, 1997)

What Do You Know About Drugs? P. Sanders and N. Myers. (Franklin Watts, 2000)

This is Ecstasy G. Thomas. (Sanctuary, 2004)

Websites

D-World (UK)
www.drugscope.org.uk/wip/24/
This special section of the informative DrugScope site is aimed at 11–14 year-olds, with clear and helpful information.

KIDS HELP LINE (Australia)
www.kidshelp.com.au
A national phone (freecall 1800 55 1800) and web-based counselling service for young people aged 5 to 18.

Ravesafe (South Africa)
www.ravesafe.org
Letters, information and advice about ecstasy and other dance drugs.

Reach Out (Australia)
www.reachout.com.au/home.asp
Provides informative and downloadable fact sheets about ecstasy and other drugs. Deals with a range of emotional issues and inspirational stories.

Talk to Frank (UK)
www.talktofrank.com/
Provides downloadable drug information for 11–14 year-olds. Helps to explain myths and offers sound advice about ecstasy and other drugs.

Urge (New Zealand)
www.whakamanawa.org.nz
Details about ecstasy and other drugs, plus other important teen issues such as alcohol, tobacco, body image and sexual matters.

Where's Your Head At? (Australia)
www.drugs.health.gov.au/youth/
A wide-ranging site aimed at young people, with detailed drug information, stories, legal advice and competitions.